First World War
and Army of Occupation
War Diary
France, Belgium and Germany

3 DIVISION
Divisional Troops
233 Machine Gun Company
1 July 1917 - 28 February 1918

WO95/1405/2

The Naval & Military Press Ltd
www.nmarchive.com
Published in association with The National Archives

Published by

The Naval & Military Press Ltd

Unit 10 Ridgewood Industrial Park,

Uckfield, East Sussex,

TN22 5QE England

Tel: +44 (0) 1825 749494

www.naval-military-press.com

www.nmarchive.com

This diary has been reprinted in facsimile from the original. Any imperfections are inevitably reproduced and the quality may fall short of modern type and cartographic standards.

© **Crown Copyright**
Images reproduced by permission of The National Archives, London, England, 2015.

Contents

Document type	Place/Title	Date From	Date To
Heading	WO95/1405/2		
Heading	War Diary of 233 Machine Gun Company Form 1-71917 To 31-7-1917 (Volume 1)		
War Diary	Belton Park	01/07/1917	12/07/1917
War Diary	Southampton	12/07/1917	12/07/1917
War Diary	Havre	13/07/1917	17/07/1917
War Diary	Buchy	17/07/1917	17/07/1917
War Diary	Bapaume	18/07/1917	18/07/1917
War Diary	Fremicourt	18/07/1917	22/07/1917
War Diary	In The Line	23/07/1917	31/07/1917
Heading	Vol 2 War Diary of 233 Machine Gun Company From 1st August 1917 To 31st August 1917		
War Diary	Fremicourt	01/08/1917	31/08/1917
Heading	War Diary of 233 Machine Gun Company 1st September 1917 to 30th September 1917 (Volume 3)		
War Diary	Beaumetz	01/09/1917	07/09/1917
War Diary	Beaulencourt	08/09/1917	18/09/1917
War Diary	Godewaersvelde	19/09/1917	19/09/1917
War Diary	Watou	20/09/1917	22/09/1917
War Diary	Mill Cott	23/09/1917	23/09/1917
War Diary	Mill Cot Frezenberg	24/09/1917	26/09/1917
War Diary	Frezenberg	26/09/1917	30/19/1917
War Diary	Ypres Potsdam Vampire	01/10/1917	01/10/1917
War Diary	Winnezeele	02/10/1917	02/10/1917
Heading	Vol 4 233rd Machine Gun Company 3rd Division For The Month Of October 1917		
War Diary	Winnezeele	03/10/1917	03/10/1917
War Diary	Ytres	04/10/1917	09/10/1917
War Diary	Ytres Favreuil	10/10/1917	13/10/1917
War Diary	Favreuil	14/10/1917	31/10/1917
Heading	War Diary of 233rd Machine Gun Company From 1st Nov 1917 To 30th Nov. 1917 Volume 5		
War Diary	Favreuil Ecoust	01/11/1917	05/11/1917
War Diary	Ecoust	05/11/1917	30/11/1917
Heading	War Diary of 233rd Machine Gun Company From 1st December 1917 To 31st December 1917 (Volume6)		
War Diary	Bullecourt	01/12/1917	31/12/1917
Heading	3rd Division Divl. Troops 233rd Machine Gun Coy. Jan-Feb 1918		
Heading	War Diary of 233rd Machine Gun Company From 1st January 1918 To 31st January 1918 (Volume7)		
War Diary	Ecoust	01/01/1918	07/01/1918
War Diary	L'Homme Mort	08/01/1918	15/01/1918
War Diary	Moyenville	16/01/1918	24/01/1918
War Diary	Henin	25/01/1918	31/01/1918
Heading	War Diary of 233rd Machine Gun Company From 1st February 1918 To 28th February 1918 (Volume 8)		
War Diary	Henin N32 A33	01/02/1918	06/02/1918
War Diary	Henin	07/02/1918	28/02/1918

30 05
14/05/2

Vol I

Confidential.

War Diary
of
233 Machine Gun Company

From 1-7-1917 to 31-7-1917

(Volume 1)

Army Form C. 2118.

WAR DIARY
or
INTELLIGENCE SUMMARY.
(Erase heading not required.)

Instructions regarding War Diaries and Intelligence Summaries are contained in F. S. Regs., Part II. and the Staff Manual respectively. Title pages will be prepared in manuscript.

Place	Date	Hour	Summary of Events and Information	Remarks and references to Appendices
Belton Park	1st July to 7th July		Under training for overseas.	
Belton Park	8th July	6PM	Orders received to proceed overseas.	
Do.	9th July		No special orders received.	
Belton Park	10th July		Orders received to entrain at Grantham Station 11th July.	
	11th July	11PM	Left Belton Park en route for overseas.	
	12th July	12.44AM	Entrained Grantham Station for overseas.	
		2.20AM	Left Grantham Station	
Southampton		11AM	Arrived Southampton Dock.	
Do.		6PM	1 Sect. & all transport left Southampton Dock. Coy divided into two portions for sea journey	
Do.		7PM	2 Sects. left on S.S. Antrim.	
Havre	13th July	9AM	S.S. Hunslet arrived "R" Hangar, Havre.	
Do.		6.30AM	Disembarked from S.S. Hunslet in S.S. Hunslet.	
Do.		7AM	S.S. Antrim arrived Havre.	
Do.		11AM	Coy arrived at rest camp.	

WAR DIARY
or
INTELLIGENCE SUMMARY.

(Erase heading not required.)

Army Form C. 2118.

Place	Date	Hour	Summary of Events and Information	Remarks and references to Appendices
HAVRE.	14th July		KIT INSPECTIONS. MOBILIZATION EQUIPMENT MADE UP TO STRENGTH AT ORDNANCE STORES.	
HAVRE	16 July	8 PM	ORDERS RECEIVED TO ENTRAIN AT GARE MARCHANDISES ON 17th JULY	
	17 July	11.20 AM	LEFT No 1A REST CAMP FOR GARE MARCHANDISES.	
	"	12.45 PM	ARRIVED GARE MARCHANDISE. ENTRAINED	
	"	4.00 PM	LEFT HAVRE.	
BUCHY	"	10 PM	ARRIVED BUCHY. TEA FOR TROOPS. ¾ HOUR HALT	
	"	9.45 PM	LEFT BUCHY	
BAPAUME	18 July	9 AM	ARRIVED BAPAUME STATION	
Do		9.30 AM	DETRAINED	
Do		10.30 AM	ORDERS RECEIVED FROM 2nd DIV. HQ TO REPORT THERE.	
		11.30 AM	LEFT BAPAUME. MARCHED TO H.Q. 2nd DIVISION.	
		11.45	MET 3rd DIV. M.G.O. ON ROAD BY RANCOURT ORDERS RECEIVED TO ENCAMP ON GROUND SOUTH OF FREMINCOURT – LEBUCQUIÈRE ROAD	

WAR DIARY
or
INTELLIGENCE SUMMARY.
(Erase heading not required.)

Army Form C. 2118.

Place	Date	Hour	Summary of Events and Information	Remarks and references to Appendices
TREMI[crossed out]COURT	18 July	1.30PM	Arrived at camping ground. Dinners / men. Tents arrived from A.S.C.	
		4.30PM	Camp pitched.	
			Reported to H.Q. 3rd Division for orders. Orders received that O.C. Coy, 1 Sect. Officers will reconnoitre the Divisional 2nd Line from Morchies through Beaumetz to Hermies.	
Do.	19 July	11 AM.	Met Div. M.G.O. & went to Morchies. Went over the 2nd Line & found gun positions	
Do.	20 July	11 AM.	Sect. & Sub. Sect. Officers & Sect. Sgt. Major went to reconnoitre their Sect. gun positions - routes for transport etc & water supply. Order received from Division that G.O.C. 3rd Div. will inspect Coy. at 12 NOON 21st July.	
Do.	21 July	12 NOON	Inspection of Company & Camp by G.O.C.	
		3 PM	[illegible]	

Army Form C. 2118.

WAR DIARY
or
INTELLIGENCE SUMMARY.
(Erase heading not required.)

Instructions regarding War Diaries and Intelligence Summaries are contained in F. S. Regs., Part II. and the Staff Manual respectively. Title pages will be prepared in manuscript.

Place	Date	Hour	Summary of Events and Information	Remarks and references to Appendices
FREMICOURT	21 July 1917	10 pm	Orders received that the Company will relieve all guns of 8th, 9th & 76th M.G. Coys in the Beaumetz – Morchies Line tomorrow 22-7-17.	
Do	22 July	2 pm	Relief orders issued to sections. Copy of orders sent to D.M.G.O.	
		8.30 pm	No 3 section moved off to relieve 2 guns of 8th M.G. Cy, 2 guns of 9th M.G. Cy.	
		8.35 pm	No 4 section moved off to relieve 4 guns of 9th M. G. Cy.	
		8.40 pm	No 2 section moved off to relieve 2 guns of 76th M.G. Cy – 2 guns of 8th M.G. Cy. Company H.Q. moved off.	
		8.45 pm	No 1 section moved off to relieve 4 guns on 76th M.G. Cy.	
		12 m.n.	Relief completed.	
Front Line	23 July		Casualty – Light Ambs. train smash whilst crossing Level crossing at Vélu. Admitted to C.C.S. Orders received D.M.G.O. Major Mackenzie assumed command of Coy.	
Front Line	23 July		No special orders received. Coy. HQ shelled in morning. 1 O.R. killed.	

A5634. Wt. W4973/M687 750,000 8/16 D. D. & L. Ltd. Forms/C.2118/13.

Army Form C. 2118.

WAR DIARY
or
INTELLIGENCE SUMMARY.
(Erase heading not required.)

Instructions regarding War Diaries and Intelligence Summaries are contained in F.S. Regs, Part II. and the Staff Manual respectively. Title pages will be prepared in manuscript.

Place	Date	Hour	Summary of Events and Information	Remarks and references to Appendices
9th Pion.	22nd July	9pm	Sections commenced to reconstruct Dugouts & build emplacements.	
Do	23rd July	do	Work continued on emplacements & dugouts. Sects at night.	
Do	24th July	9pm	Work continued on emplacements.	
Do.	25th July	9pm	New emplacements made for 2 emplacements. Sections visited.	
Do	26th July	9pm	New emplacements finished. Sects visited.	
Do	27th July	9pm	Dugouts near gun positions. Traps for 2 other 8 guns. Sects visited.	
Do	28th July	9pm	Sections visited.	
Do	29th July	9pm	Nothing of interest to report. Sects visited.	
Do	30th July		1 O.R. joined Coy to complete establishment. Coy. hayed for first time after arriving in France.	
Do.	31st July	12 noon	Orders issued to Sects to change gun positions. No 1 changing of position completed.	

Burnt

Vol 2

War Diary
of
233 Machine Gun Company.

From 1st August 1917 — To 31st August 1917.

Edward Gardner Capt for
I. Comdg. No. 233 Machine Gun Coy.

Instructions regarding War Diaries and Intelligence Summaries are contained in F. S. Regs., Part II. and the Staff Manual respectively. Title pages will be prepared in manuscript.

WAR DIARY
or
~~INTELLIGENCE SUMMARY~~.
(Erase heading not required.)

Army Form C. 2118.

Place	Date	Hour	Summary of Events and Information	Remarks and references to Appendices
FREMICOURT	August 1st		[illegible] to repeat today. [illegible] the line.	[illegible]
	2nd		Orders received that the [illegible] guns [illegible] the 1st [illegible] would [illegible] [illegible] shortly by the 62nd Division.	[illegible]
	3rd		O.C. Coy reconnoitred line on the left. Orders issued that the 4 right hand guns would be relieved next day by 62 Division. 1 O.R. to hospital	[illegible]
	4th		Relief of 4 right guns complete 9.15 pm	[illegible]
	5th		Quiet all day. Enemy [illegible] [illegible]	[illegible]
	6th		Operation Orders issued to [illegible] [illegible] take over 4 positions on left [illegible] from the 201st [illegible] Coy. Relief complete 11.15 pm	[illegible]
	7th		Instructions received that 1 Officer would join the Coy shortly.	[illegible]
	8th		Orders received that only 8 guns would be [illegible] [illegible] issued to [illegible].	[illegible]

A5834 Wt. W4973/M687 750,000 8/16 D. D. & L. Ltd. Forms/C.2118/13.

Army Form C. 2118.

WAR DIARY
or
INTELLIGENCE SUMMARY.
(Erase heading not required.)

Instructions regarding War Diaries and Intelligence Summaries are contained in F.S. Regs., Part II. and the Staff Manual respectively. Title pages will be prepared in manuscript.

Place	Date	Hour	Summary of Events and Information	Remarks and references to Appendices
[illegible]	9th		2nd Rest. W.A Regt Hand over to [illegible] [illegible] [illegible] [illegible] Relief 8y - 11.02 a.m. to a to b a.m. Completed 11.15 PM	
	10th		Very quiet. Letter to report	
	11th		Day quiet. Made a patrol — a model of sight	
	12th		Very quiet. Letter to report	
	13th		Day quiet. letter [illegible]	
	14th		Quiet. Health & [illegible]	
	15th		10 P.R. [illegible] Enemy [illegible] [illegible] [illegible] 9 O.R. on outpost	
	16th		[illegible] [illegible]	
	17th		10 P.R. [illegible] sent [illegible] [illegible] 1 O.R. over left knee	
	18th		Quiet all day	

Army Form C. 2118.

WAR DIARY
or
INTELLIGENCE SUMMARY.
(Erase heading not required.)

Place	Date	Hour	Summary of Events and Information	Remarks and references to Appendices
PREMONT	17	7.0.0	[illegible]	
	2			
		12 noon		
		1 AM		
	2			
	14			

Army Form C. 2118.

WAR DIARY
or
INTELLIGENCE SUMMARY.
(Erase heading not required.)

Instructions regarding War Diaries and Intelligence Summaries are contained in F. S. Regs., Part II. and the Staff Manual respectively. Title pages will be prepared in manuscript.

Place	Date	Hour	Summary of Events and Information	Remarks and references to Appendices
FRENCHE			[illegible handwritten entries]	

W3.

Confidential

War Diary
of
233 Machine Gun Company

from 1st September 1917 to 30th September 1917

(Volume 3)

WAR DIARY
or
INTELLIGENCE SUMMARY.
(Erase heading not required.)

Army Form C. 2118.

Place	Date	Hour	Summary of Events and Information	Remarks and references to Appendices
BEAUMETZ	19.17 Sept.	1	Orders received that Division would be relieved shortly. Quiet all along line	L.P. Jeff.
		2	Quiet all day	L.P. Jeff
		3	O/Os No 9 moved that No 1 & No 2 sections in the line would be relieved by 193 M.G. Coy & that the details camp would also be taken over on the 6th inst.	L.P. Jeff
		4	Nothing of importance. O.C. 193 M.G. Coy came to reconnoitre the line	L.P. Jeff
		5	C.H.Q. moved from the line to Details Camp	L.P. Jeff
		6	Nos 3 & 4 Sections & Transport moved to BEAUENCOURT in the morning. In the evening nos 1 & 2 Sections were relieved by 193 Coy in the line – Relief Compte 10·45 p.m. – No 5 & No 2 arrived camp about 1·30 A.M.	L.P. Jeff
		7	2nd Lt. S. Field was appointed Adjutant and 2nd I/C.	L.P. Jeff

Army Form C.2118.

WAR DIARY
or
INTELLIGENCE SUMMARY.

(Erase heading not required.)

Place	Date	Hour	Summary of Events and Information	Remarks and references to Appendices
BEAULENCOURT	8. Sept 1917		Company Training.	1.9.17.
	9 "		Warning order received re next move	2.9.17.
	10 "		Company Training	2.9.17.
	11 "		do	1.9.17.
	12 "		do	1.9.17.
	13 "		do	2.9.17.
	14 "		do Orders received that Company would be under orders of 76th Bde for move - Entraining Stations allotted.	2.9.17.
	15 "		Coy Training.	1.9.17.
	16 "		do do. Orders received to entrain BAPAUME WEST on the 18th inst at 2-30 pm.	1.9.17.
	17 "		Preparations made for move	1.9.17.
	18 "		Marched out of camp 1pm Entrained BAPAUME WEST and left at 5-30 p.m.	1.9.17.

WAR DIARY or INTELLIGENCE SUMMARY

Army Form C.2118.

Place	Date	Hour	Summary of Events and Information	Remarks and references to Appendices
GODEWAERSVELDT	19. Sept. 17	3.30 A.M.	Arrived at GODEWAERSVELDE at 3.30 A.M. marched off to camp at TRAPPIST FARM between ABEELE & WATOU about 8 miles	19.9.17
WATOU	20.		Company training.	20.9.17
	21.		Company training. O.C. Coy with D.M.G.O. reconnoitred line in front of FREZENBERG RIDGE.	6.9.17
	22.		Company training. O.C. Coy & two officers reconnoitred line & routes to line. Preparations made to move.	22.9.17
MILL Cot.	23.		Transport left camp at 12 noon. Part of the transport went to details camp at H7A 2.1. BRANDHOEK remaining behind. S.A.A. Limbers moved up to just this side of FREZENBERG RIDGE and dumped all Gun equipment &c. The Coy left at 7 P.M. m Motor buses returned at dump about 10.45 p.m. Reliefs started autochious moved up to positions with pack mules. Very hard going on the track was swept with shell fire.	23.9.17 23.9.17

Army Form C. 2118.

WAR DIARY
or
INTELLIGENCE SUMMARY.
(Erase heading not required.)

Place	Date	Hour	Summary of Events and Information	Remarks and references to Appendices
MILL Cot. FREZENBERG	1917 24 Sept.		Company got into position at about 3.30 AM having barraged extremely well. Casualties here 2nd Lt. E.A. KNIGHT and 2nd Lt. R.C. JACKSON killed other casualties were 3 O.R. killed and 7 O.R. wounded. Nos 1.2.+4 Sections were at POTSDAM and VAMPIR No 3 Sect. in reserve behind FREZENBERG RIDGE.	19a/r
	25.		Details camp moved To camp 16. II B c. 8.9. Nos 1.2+4 sections were having a fresh/natatoria. No 4 section have had their guns buried twice and S.A.A. blown up etc. No 1 have had their bottoms blown away as well. Casualties to-day were 1 O.R. wounded and 1 O.R. wounded yesterday died of wounds.	Sept
	26.		The attack started at 5.50 AM Nos 1 & 2 4th sections barraged from that hour to 8.5 A.M. No 3 section stood by - The barrage went off very well they two fired perfectly. R.H. de	19 a/r

WAR DIARY
or
INTELLIGENCE SUMMARY.

(Erase heading not required.)

Army Form C. 2118.

Place	Date	Hour	Summary of Events and Information	Remarks and references to Appendices
FREZENBERG (Sheet?) 28.b."	Sept. 17 26."		However the enemy fire seemed to find us + the sections had a very bad time. In the evening the S.O.S. went up and the guns fired — No 4 sect had been badly shelled during the afternoon and had been twice turned again. No 3 section moved up to positions about 1000 x in front of POTSDAM. Casualties today were. 7 other ranks wounded.	2.p.m. 10.p.m.
do.	27."		It had quietened down today but the enemy guns are fairly active at times. No: 1 2 + 4 sections have held on splendidly and have shown a considerable amount of ground about. No 3 section (2 Teams) moved to a position in the front line at VAN ISACKERS FARM	10p/2h 10.p.m.

Army Form C. 2118.

WAR DIARY
or
INTELLIGENCE SUMMARY.
(Erase heading not required.)

Instructions regarding War Diaries and Intelligence
Summaries are contained in F.S. Regs., Part II.
and the Staff Manual respectively. Title pages
will be prepared in manuscript.

Place	Date	Hour	Summary of Events and Information	Remarks and references to Appendices
FREZENBERG	Sept 17 27		Casualties to-day were: 5 O.R. wounded 1 O.R. missing.	J.P.zh.
do.	28.		The Enemy were fairly Quiet in the morning but put down a heavy barrage at midday and about 6.30 p.m. The Enemy shelled all in & around Frezenport. No Reflection were heavily shelled in the Evening. Casualties Nil.	J.P.zh.
do.	29.		The Enemy were fairly quiet in the morning but in the Evening 2.30 p.m. over the Company lines. H.Q.s dropped bombs and caused considerable damage. Casualties to-day: 2nd Lt. V.A.R. King and 1 O.R. Killed. Orders received 3.10 p.m. that the Company would be relieved by the 23rd Aus. Div. M.G. Coy on night of 30th / 1st Oct.	J.P.zh.

Place	Date	Hour	Summary of Events and Information	Remarks and references to Appendices
FREZENBERG	Sept 30 1917		The Company should have been relieved at 8.30 p.m by the 23rd Australian Tun. Co but remained in until the following morning.	J Reid 2/Lt R.E O.C 233 M.C.

Army Form C. 2118.

WAR DIARY
or
INTELLIGENCE SUMMARY.
(Erase heading not required.)

Place	Date	Hour	Summary of Events and Information	Remarks and references to Appendices
YPRES	1917 1 Oct		3rd Div BO186 received re move to WINNEZEELE. Company should have been relieved at 2.30 p.m. 30th Oct. but this did not take	
POTSDAM VAMPIRE			place until 3 a.m. The bivouac would take BAVARIA HOUSE from 8 p.m. Relieve Thorough.	
			Left subsection (No 3 Sec) were not relieved until following day.	
			Casualties wounded 4 O.R. Wounded remained upon as 2 O.R. 4 mls wld	
			Company entrained (less one subjection) at BRANDHOEK transport to WINNEZEELE. Transport less fire limbs by Road.	
WINNEZEELE	2 Oct	6 pm	Gun cleaning checking & motilization equipment. Subsect: 8/No 3 Sec. arrived at camp.	
do	3 Oct		Div Bo 188 9th mtn Bde O.O 145 } reference movements to ins received. 76th Inf Bde Bde OO 5.	
		AM 6.30	Transport left by Road 6.30 to 8. Orst arrived 3 pm	
		9.30 PM 11.30	Company entrained at WINNEZEELE Bo Comen. Company entrained	

233rd MACHINE GUN COMPANY 3rd DIVISION.

WAR DIARY FOR THE MONTH OF

OCTOBER 1917

WAR DIARY
or
INTELLIGENCE SUMMARY.

(Erase heading not required.)

Army Form C. 2118.

Place	Date	Hour	Summary of Events and Information	Remarks and references to Appendices
WINNEZEELE	3 Oct		Evacuations 2 O.R. Sick. Reinforcement 1 O.R. rejoined 3 O.R. from Army Base	
YTRES	4 Oct		Arrived BAPAUME West 6 a.m. detrained, marched to Camp at YTRES	
do	5 Oct		1 O.R. Wounded Sick. Under Canvas Very wet	
do	6 Oct		Coy training - Very wet	
do	7 Oct		Div Op/89 received warning Order to relieve 201 M.G.Cy in BULLECOURT deciso on 10/11 th	
do	8 Oct		2nd Lt. A.E.S. Browne + 2/Lt H.L. Thomas (and Coy Sm Roll) Coy O.O. No 6 moved re relief.	
do	9 Oct		O.C. Coy + 2 Officers went to reconnoitre position at ECOUST 1 O.R. Evacuated Sick.	

Army Form C. 2118.

WAR DIARY
or
INTELLIGENCE SUMMARY.
(Erase heading not required.)

Instructions regarding War Diaries and Intelligence Summaries are contained in F. S. Regs., Part II and the Staff Manual respectively. Title pages will be prepared in manuscript.

Place	Date	Hour	Summary of Events and Information	Remarks and references to Appendices
YTRES FAVREUIL	10 Oct	A.M. 9.30	Transport moved by Road to FAVREUIL to Camp No 25 arrived 11.30 p.m.	
		10.0	Company entrained at YTRES arrived FAVREUIL 12 noon. Camp shared with 201 M.G.Coy. in knicker.	
		5 p.m	No 1 & 2 Section moved up to ECOUST and relieved 2 sections of 201 M.G.Coy	J. Frank Appt
			Relief complete 8.45 P.m.	
			2nd Lt. H.C. GESSE joined Coy from Base	
			Situation in line quiet.	
	11 Oct		201 M.G.Coy. left camp.	
			Situation quiet.	1 Rudolph Appt
			Lecture Running.	
	12 Oct		2 Lt. T.S. ROBSON Joined Coy from Base as Transport Officer	
			Reinforcements 1 O.R. Cowie	
			Situation in line quiet.	25 Regd X Pct
	13 Oct		Very little. Situation quiet	1 Re Inf Kty

WAR DIARY
or
INTELLIGENCE SUMMARY.

(Erase heading not required.)

Army Form C. 2118.

Place	Date	Hour	Summary of Events and Information	Remarks and references to Appendices
FAVREUIL	14 Oct		Section Ramny at Details Camp. Situation in line quiet.	1 Field Amb Aty
do	15 Oct		Section Ramny at Details Camp. Guns No 6 35 A(1) No 7 35 (A2) No 8 35(A1) fired in targets from Zero to Zero +45 co-operated in M/Guns 9/16"KRR… Casualties 1 O.R. accidentally wounded. Evacuated.	1 Field Amb Aty
do	16 Oct		2nd R.B. F. Ange moved into front line. Situation in line quiet. Evacuation 1 O.R. sick, 1 Cpl on course to England. Reinforcements 1 O.R. arrn.	1 Field Amb Aty
do	17 Oct		Section Ramny at Details Camp. Reinforcements 11 mules 2 Horses. Situation in line quiet.	1 Field Amb Aty

Army Form C. 2118.

WAR DIARY
or
INTELLIGENCE SUMMARY.
(Erase heading not required.)

Instructions regarding War Diaries and Intelligence Summaries are contained in F. S. Regs., Part II. and the Staff Manual respectively. Title pages will be prepared in manuscript.

Place	Date	Hour	Summary of Events and Information	Remarks and references to Appendices
FAVREUIL	18 Oct		Section training + details. Weather fine. Situation in line quiet.	J. Reed 7th A/H
do.	19 Oct		do.	J. Reed 7th A/H
			Appointments 2 O/R to be head of spreads (unpaid) Reinforcements 6 O.R. from Base	
do.	20 Oct		Coys O/O. nos. Coy O/O. nos. moved to relief. No 4 left relieved No 3 Sect. No 2 left subsection relieved No 1 left subsection — No 1 Reinforcements remaining in line — Relief complete 8hrs. Situation Quiet	J. Reed 7th A/H
do.	21 Oct		Weather fine. Situation quiet. Right subsection No 2 + No 5 ТР по perimetre N. west of NOREUIL at 8.30 pm. Right subsection hon. withdrew at 9.30 pm.	J. Reed 7th A/H
do.	22 Oct		Section training at camp — Weather cold. Situation in line quiet. Reinforcements 14 O.R. from Base.	J. Reed 7th A/H

Army Form C. 2118.

WAR DIARY
or
INTELLIGENCE SUMMARY.
(Erase heading not required.)

Instructions regarding War Diaries and Intelligence Summaries are contained in F. S. Regs., Part II. and the Staff Manual respectively. Title pages will be prepared in manuscript.

Place	Date	Hour	Summary of Events and Information	Remarks and references to Appendices
FAVREUIL	23 Oct		Lecture training at Details Camp. Weather fine. Situation in line quiet.	
do	24 Oct		do. Evacuations 1 O.R. (D.U.) sick. Reinforcements 2 3 O.R. from base.	
do	25 Oct		Right subsector no 2 moved back to positions previously occupied by 1 Bns. right subsector Wm. at COAST strongpoints. Subsector quiet.	
do	26 Oct		Weather improves. 1 O.R. rejoined from R.A.S.E. Situation quiet. Promotions & appointments: 2 Cpls to be A/Sgts, 2 L/Cpls n/pd to be Cpls, acting Corporal, 3 unpaid L/Cpls to be paid acting L/Cpls.	

Army Form C. 2118.

WAR DIARY
or
INTELLIGENCE SUMMARY.
(Erase heading not required.)

Place	Date	Hour	Summary of Events and Information	Remarks and references to Appendices
FAVREUIL	27 Oct.		Lecture Training at Details Camp. Situation quiet. 3 Military Medals awarded to Company.	1st Reserve Regt
do	29 Oct.		Section Training. Situation quiet.	1st Reserve Regt
do	29 Oct.		do do	1st Reserve Regt
			Reinforcements. 1 O.R. rejoined T.O.R. joined from Base.	
do	30 Oct.		Section Training. Situation quiet. 1 O.R. rejoined from leave 17.11.12.	1st Reserve Regt
do	31 Oct.		Section Training. Situation quiet. Weather fine.	1st Reserve Regt

Confidential

War Diary
of
233rd Machine Gun Company

From 1st Nov. 1917. 2. 30th Nov. 1917.

Volume 5.

WAR DIARY
or
INTELLIGENCE SUMMARY

Army Form C. 2118.

Place	Date	Hour	Summary of Events and Information	Remarks and references to Appendices
FAVREUIL ECOUST	1st Nov.		3rd Div. S.S.G 28/19 Received reference Barrage on Z day. Sections 1 & 3 went up 16 chg emplacements at C.4.0. Sunken road. Situation quiet.	S. Booth
	2 Nov.		Sections 1 & 3 continued work at Sunken Road and remained at ECOUST. Rounds fired 13500 at enemy gaps in wire at S4.9. Evacuations 2 O.R. 1 & C.S. deep	S. Booth
	3 Nov.		In the company in the field and at ECOUST proper, our work in sunken road and back H.Q in NOREUIL-LONGATTE RD	S. Beeroth
	4 Nov.		Nos 1 & 3 sections returned to camp nearly all work completed at rendezvous. Situation in line. Fired 10,000 rounds at enemy gaps in wire	S. Beeroth
	5 Nov.		Section having a stand. Foggy weather. Situation in line quiet 13,000 rounds fired at gaps in wire. See Lt. C.T. Smith awarded M.C. See Lt. D.F.S. Provose left by for Base Depot - Evacuations 1 Off. 1 O.R. 1 & C.S. deep	S. Beeroth

WAR DIARY
or
INTELLIGENCE SUMMARY.

Army Form C. 2118.

Instructions regarding War Diaries and Intelligence Summaries are contained in F.S. Regs., Part II. and the Staff Manual respectively. Title pages will be prepared in manuscript.

(Erase heading not required.)

Place	Date	Hour	Summary of Events and Information	Remarks and references to Appendices
ECOUST.	5 Nov. Cont.d		3rd. Div: S.S.G. 28/20 reference M.G. Organization in Barrage. 3rd. Div. S.S.G. 28/21 reference 2.S.G. 28/17 cancelled and New Disposition of Batteries	J. Rudolf
	6 Nov.		Lecture training and details Camp Improvements. Situation in line Quiet. Rounds Fired 9500.	J. Rudolf
	7 Nov.		Coy 0/0.12. Relief of Nos 2 & Lee. C. Nos 1 & 3 Coys. Relief complete 7.15 p.m. Reinforcements 2 O.R. from B.A.F. 3rd.Div. S.S.G. 28/26 received Amendments to Para 6 S.S.G. 28/21	J. Rudolf
	8 Nov.		Fatigue party making S.A.A. Dumps at Back H.Q. Lecture training and details. Reinforcements 4 O.R. from Base Evacuations 3 to C.C.S. sick	J. Rudolf

Army Form C.2118.

WAR DIARY
or
INTELLIGENCE SUMMARY.
(Erase heading not required.)

Instructions regarding War Diaries and Intelligence Summaries are contained in F.S. Regs., Part II and the Staff Manual respectively. Title pages will be prepared in manuscript.

Place	Date	Hour	Summary of Events and Information	Remarks and references to Appendices
ECOUST	9 Nov		Weather very wet. Evacuations 1 O.R. to C.S. sick. Promotions & appointments 2/Lpl Wilkinson H.H. to be Actg Corpl from 4.10.17. 3rd S.W. S.S.G. 28/32. Addendum to instructions No.8. A.P.G. 28/2. " A/3173. Pivot Arrangements.	A. Receipts
	10 Nov		Fine day. Section training and details. Situation in line quiet. Rounds fired 15325 at Sapr in Moe Sningp. N.G.	A. Receipts
	11 Nov		Work on Dumps. Back H.Q. completed. Stand fast. Rounds fired 15,500 at Sapr in Moe Sningp. Enemy H.Q. Dinalow Gues. Evacuations 1 O.R. to C.S. sick.	A. Receipts
	12 Nov		Fine sunny day. Section training and details. Situation in line quiet. Rounds fired 26,000 & same targets. Promotions & appointments. The following approved/appointed 2e/Lpl Knowlton Dale E.T. (M.M.) 99926 Pte Weydouville G.E. N/Divison of Regt 102857 . Morgan J.	A. Receipts

Army Form C. 2118.

WAR DIARY
or
INTELLIGENCE SUMMARY.
(Erase heading not required.)

Instructions regarding War Diaries and Intelligence Summaries are contained in F. S. Regs., Part II. and the Staff Manual respectively. Title pages will be prepared in manuscript.

Place	Date	Hour	Summary of Events and Information	Remarks and references to Appendices
ECOUST	13 Nov		Weather fine. Lewis training and Details. Situation in line quiet - Rounds fired 9500 at Sap in enemy front N.9.	Recd 4/5
	14 Nov.		Weather fine. Lewis training and details. Situation in line quiet. Rounds fired 5320 at same target.	Recd 4/5
	15 Nov.		Coy C/O B moved - Instructions to Section re Barrage on Z day. Section training and Details.	
			Weather fine. Situation in line quiet. Rounds fired 6700. Evacuations 1 O.R. to C.C. Stn.	Recd 4/5
	16 Nov.		Section Training and Details - Weather fine. Situation in line quiet. Rounds fired 6200. Advance party 2 w/o Lt's returned here. 3 NSW: A/3/73/2 received.	Recd 4/5

Army Form C.2118.

WAR DIARY
or
INTELLIGENCE SUMMARY.
(Erase heading not required.)

Instructions regarding War Diaries and Intelligence Summaries are contained in F. S. Regs., Part II. and the Staff Manual respectively. Title pages will be prepared in manuscript.

Place	Date	Hour	Summary of Events and Information	Remarks and references to Appendices
ECOUST.	17 Nov.		Section Training & Details. Weather fine. Remaining sections of 240 Coy arrived in Camp. Evacuations 1 O.R. 15th C.C.S. Sick 1 O.R. To Base for a course. S.S.G. 25/59. Fire orders reviewed.	A. Reid 2/Lt
	18 Nov.		Preparations for Move to two. Situation in line quiet. Evacuation 1 O.R. 15th C.C.S. Reinforcements 1 O.R. from Base	A. Reid 2/Lt
	19 Nov.		Y day. Company reoccupied position in Sunken Road C & D. C.H.Q. dugout TT BULLECOURT. Back C.H.Q. Sunken road NOREUIL - ECOUST. Weather cold. Dark Night some rain. Evacuations 1 O.R. 15th C.C.S. sick.	A. Reid 2/Lt
	20 Nov.		Z Day Zero hour 6.20 A.M. C. & D Batteries fired 71,550 rounds to Noon in their Barrage lines. Weather misty & cold.	A. Reid 2/Lt

A5834 Wt.W4973/M687 750,000 8/16 D.D.&L.Ltd. Forms/C.2118/13.

WAR DIARY
or
INTELLIGENCE SUMMARY.
(Erase heading not required.)

Army Form C. 2118.

Instructions regarding War Diaries and Intelligence Summaries are contained in F.S. Regs., Part II. and the Staff Manual respectively. Title pages will be prepared in manuscript.

Place	Date	Hour	Summary of Events and Information	Remarks and references to Appendices
ECOUST	21.Nov.		Weather. Wet storm. C & D Batteries fired 68-250 rounds per hour. Reinforcement 1 O.R. returned from C.R.S.	W.H.H.
	22.Nov.		3rd Div. G.S. 197/37. 240 Company withdrawn from line. No 4 Sec & Subsection No 3 moved to SYDNEY CROSS as D1 Battery. Subsection No 3 15TA1 Battery in RAILWAY RESERVE. C & D Batteries fired 22,750 Rounds per hour. Weather cold. Evacuations - P.O.R. Sick to F.A.	J. Rudolph
	23.Nov.		3rd Div. G.S. 197/40. Programme of fire for 24th inst. Rounds fired Nil. Weather changeable - cold.	J. Rudolph
	24.Nov.		3rd Div. G.S. 197/41. Programme of fire. D. Battery fired 13,500 D.1. 10,750 rounds.	J. Rudolph

WAR DIARY
or
INTELLIGENCE SUMMARY.

(Erase heading not required.)

Army Form C. 2118.

Place	Date	Hour	Summary of Events and Information	Remarks and references to Appendices
ECOUST	Nov. 25		76 Infy Bde O/o. Photo. reference slip	
			D. Battery fired 16000	
			D¹ " " 1500	
			A.¹ " " 375 D.	J. Reid?
	26.		D. Battery fired 12000	
			A¹ " " 8000	
			Company withdrew from Battery positions - 9/m 2 M Board lecturing took	
			up positions in ECOUST LINE previously expressed	
			Nos 1 & 3 returned to Camp at FAVREUIL	
			The Company's gun fire 225,750 rounds.	
			Reinforcements C.Q.M.S. Forman - from 105 M.G. Coy	J. Reids?
	27.		Situation in line - ECOUST shelled fairly heavily.	
			Evacuation 1. O.R. (C.Q.M.S. Rowson) to 2nd coy as C.S.W.	J. Reids?

Army Form C. 2118.

WAR DIARY
or
INTELLIGENCE SUMMARY.
(Erase heading not required.)

Instructions regarding War Diaries and Intelligence Summaries are contained in F. S. Regs., Part II. and the Staff Manual respectively. Title pages will be prepared in manuscript.

Place	Date	Hour	Summary of Events and Information	Remarks and references to Appendices
ECOUST	28 Nov.		Situation in line somewhere of RAILWAY RESERVE one gun shots	
			Act Struck Shrapnel.	
			Rounds fired 5450.	
			Appointments. 9999 to Pte Jackson J.D. to be acting R/Sgt (unpaid) from 29th inst.	1 Recd
	29.		O.C. Coy. - (Capt. J.H. Desfoux). and Lieut. T. Snow went over to N.N.	1 Recd
			Rounds fired 18600 at Saps in Nos Pincery H.Q.	1 Recd
	30		Section raining at Detruis	1 Recd
			Rounds fired 13650 - at Copse TRENCH - SUNKEN ROAD U.15.a.00. 2 Recd

Confidential

War Diary
of
233rd Machine Gun Company

(Volume 6)

From 1st December 1917   To 31st December 1917

WAR DIARY
INTELLIGENCE SUMMARY

Army Form C. 2118.

Place	Date	Hour	Summary of Events and Information	Remarks and references to Appendices
VILLERS BRETT	15 Dec.		Still standing to ready to take up defensive position. 11,000 rounds fired at various targets. Defensive patrols out. Various casualties. 1 O.R. evacuated.	
"	16		Cay. O.O. No 13 issued (copy attached) Situation quiet.	
"	17		Inspection of the line deemed by the Staff too late. The day heavy shelling at C' Coy H.Q. Consequently the shelling at our detachments with difficulty getting out 7,000 rounds fired at various targets.	
"	18		Situation still at about 11.25 rounds fired at various targets. 1 Pte evacuated.	
"	19		Situation general. Various minimum targets. 1 O.R. evacuated. Wounded (gas shell) — 7,150 rounds fired at course at CACHIERS	
"	20		Battery interest after having quiet nite. 1 Officer & 2 O.Rs evacuated with influenza. Battery Cmdr LI-Col A Rouse DSO 2 Rounds of various kinds of ammunition fired. No casualties.	

WAR DIARY or INTELLIGENCE SUMMARY

Army Form C.2118.

Place	Date	Hour	Summary of Events and Information	Remarks and references to Appendices
Rullecourt	7th		Very quiet + wet. Our section out of the line continue training	
	8th		Getting S[ection] out to get.	
	9th		Getting S[ection] intact to get.	
	10th		Very quiet. the line. Orders received to standby to be ready to reinforce line if attacked.	
	11th		Status. line unaltered.	
	12th		Very heavy barrage by enemy at 6.30 A.M. At 9 A.M. Line – Point du Jour – Gilles – N° REUIL – ECOUST Road. Enemy attacked & managed to enter our line at B.H. Coy Sqn Counter attack launched & regained original position. At 1 P.M. we held a line from the railway to S.O.S. on 7 1990 N of PTS evacuated during attack.	

WAR DIARY

INTELLIGENCE SUMMARY

Army Form C. 2118.

Instructions regarding War Diaries and Intelligence Summaries are contained in F.S. Regs., Part II. and the Staff Manual respectively. Title pages will be prepared in manuscript.

Place	Date	Hour	Summary of Events and Information	Remarks and references to Appendices
BULLECOURT	13th		Violent enemy fire. Early morning. Enemy did 0.5" attack Railway Triangle 203. Believed to be enemy transport line to BULLERS. Round about 18000 a SOS sent up by 1st Yorks & Lancs. Regt. left of battn. No reports immediately.	
	14th		Artillery ordered back to station.	
	15th		B.O. Orr returned from ongoing. B.O. Waggs back to ongoing. 150 recruits to attack this afternoon Cavalry 5 tanks to consolidate front under SOS line.	
	16th		Situation [illegible] quietr. Waggs line crossed to ongoing. Tanks did not arrive. 1 O.R. evacuated sick.	
	17th		1 hun on consulate withdrawn & placed in mud in night Casualties withdrawn from Coys. Platoon to consolidate attack from reserve field at [illegible] the SOS. 1 OR evacuated sick.	

WAR DIARY

INTELLIGENCE SUMMARY

(Erase heading not required.)

Army Form C. 2118.

Place	Date	Hour	Summary of Events and Information	Remarks and references to Appendices
Villecourt	12		Very quiet to the line. 2/Lt. L.A. EAGES joined the coy. from the base	
"	13		Very quiet in the line. 1 O.R. evacuated sick. 2,000 rounds fired at aeroplanes	
"	14		Very quiet. the line. 2000 rounds fired at enemy aeroplanes	
"	15		Very quiet in the line. 3000 rounds fired at enemy aircraft. 3 O.R. evacuated sick	
"	16		Very quiet in line. nothing to report. Fired a lot of rounds nightly at enemy aircraft.	
"	17		Back area attacked by enemy aircraft (Chipilly area) Situation line quiet. Heavy bombing at night by enemy aircraft	
"	18		Very quiet. 3rd July 00,00,00,08 rounds 3rd gun fired at enemy. Situation line quiet. At night heavy bombing by enemy aircraft on villages	
	19			

WAR DIARY
INTELLIGENCE SUMMARY

(Erase heading not required.)

Army Form C. 2118.

Place	Date	Hour	Summary of Events and Information	Remarks and references to Appendices
Hullecourt	22nd		[illegible handwritten entries]	

3RD DIVISION
DIVL. TROOPS

233RD MACHINE GUN COY.

JAN-FEB 1918.

Confidential

War Diary

of

233rd Machine Gun Company.

From 1st January 1918. To. 31st January 1918.

Army Form C. 2118.

WAR DIARY
or
INTELLIGENCE SUMMARY.
(Erase heading not required.)

Instructions regarding War Diaries and Intelligence Summaries are contained in F.S. Regs., Part II. and the Staff Manual respectively. Title pages will be prepared in manuscript.

Place	Date	Hour	Summary of Events and Information	Remarks and references to Appendices
ECOUST.	1918 1 Jany		Keen frost. Situation quiet. Capt J.H. Des Voeux to LAHAMEUX on 3 days course.	J. Reidh
	2 Jany		Rain - Subject of No 5 revised hy direction 1/11/17. 40 Divn. No 1055/20 (G) received reference relieving 121 Coy in BULLECOURT sector	J. Reidh
	3 Jany		Situation Normal. Section training at Details Evacuation 1 N.C.O. to C.C.S.	J. Reidh
	4 Jany		Capt J.H. Des Voeux returned from LAHAMEUX Weather cold with some snow	J. Reidh
	5 Jany		Reinforcements 1 D.R. (Signaller) from Base Situation Normal - Weather fine.	J. Reidh
	6 Jany		do. Evacuation 1. O. R. to C.C.S.	J. Reidh

Army Form C. 2118.

WAR DIARY
or
INTELLIGENCE SUMMARY.
(Erase heading not required.)

Instructions regarding War Diaries and Intelligence Summaries are contained in F. S. Regs., Part II. and the Staff Manual respectively. Title pages will be prepared in manuscript.

Place	Date	Hour	Summary of Events and Information	Remarks and references to Appendices
ECOUST	7 Jany		Coy O/D. No 19. reference relief of 121 M.G. Coy carried out. Dispositions as follows: No 1. Sect. 2 guns. D.27.D.3570. No 2 Sec. 4 guns in Railway Reserve + Tank Avenue. No 3 Sec. 2 guns in BULLECOURT 2 guns Tower Support. No 4 Sec in South Road C.4.A. 2 Sec in ECOUST defence line - 2 guns. Coy H.Q. "L'Homme Mort". Lt. Reid returned from leave.	L. Reid
L'HOMME MORT.	8 Jany		S.O.S. went up at 6.30. A.M. Guns fired 6000 Rounds. Enemy penetrated into TANK SUPPORT but were subsequently ejected with loss of 15 Prisoners. Snow fell during the day.	L. Reid
"	9 Jany		Fine Cold morning changing to sleet & rain later. Situation quiet. Rounds fired on Bullech Ave. 5250 on heightened S.O.S. lines 11750.	L. Reid

A 5834 Wt. W4973/M687 750,000 8/16 D. D. & L. Ltd. Forms/C.2118/13.

Army Form C. 2118.

WAR DIARY
or
INTELLIGENCE SUMMARY.
(Erase heading not required.)

Instructions regarding War Diaries and Intelligence Summaries are contained in F. S. Regs., Part II. and the Staff Manual respectively. Title pages will be prepared in manuscript.

Place	Date	Hour	Summary of Events and Information	Remarks and references to Appendices
L'HOMME MORT	10 Jan		Weather fine & warmer. Situation Normal except for M.G. activity. Rounds fired on S.O.S. Lines Ostrich Trench & Stenfish 35350. Evacuations 1 O.R. to Hospital in U.K.	L. Field
	11 "		Rain. No 3 Section had one gun at C. post put out of action by Enemy M.G. Fire Rounds fired 44250 on Ostrich trench & Stenfish. Evacuations - 1 O.R. to C.C.S.	L. Field
	12 "		Weather colder - fine - Situation Normal. Rounds fired 17000. 3rd Div: 0/0210. Reference relief by 8th M. Gloy. Reinforcements 3 Bns. Evacuation 1 O.R. to C.C.S.	L. Field
	13 "		Frosty. Fine day. No 2 Section in Railway Reserve put out of action by Enemy M.G. Bullet Enemy shelling in rear of ECOUST all day. 121 Bde 745/66 (A) received reference relief in line by 21 M. Gloy Reinforcements 9 O.R. from 76 M. G. Coy	L. Field

M3534 H.W.W.4973M687 750,000 8/16 D. D. & L. Ltd. Forms/C.2118/13.

Army Form C. 2118.

WAR DIARY
or
INTELLIGENCE SUMMARY.

(Erase heading not required.)

Instructions regarding War Diaries and Intelligence Summaries are contained in F. S. Regs., Part II. and the Staff Manual respectively. Title pages will be prepared in manuscript.

Place	Date	Hour	Summary of Events and Information	Remarks and references to Appendices
L'HOMME-MORT	10 & 14 day		FINE DAY. Situation Quiet. Rounds fired on which No. 13,000 Reinforcement 1 O.R. reported from Kite Hospital. Marched two I.O.R. to C.C.S.	
	15 day		Very Wet. Coy 070.20. Rept Lys: 21, M.G. Coy. covered wet	
MOYENVILLE	16 day		Moved to MOYEN CAMP MOYENVILLE. Rein. forcements 9 O.R. from Base. Evacuations 1 O.R. to C.C.S.	
"	17 day		Cleaning up in Camp. Lce/t. W.L. JAMS left on leave to U.K.	
"	18 day		Raining all Day- men working inside camp.	
"	19 day		Company training-	
"	20 day		Fine weather. Company training in morning. Church Service in Camp in afternoon.	

Army Form C. 2118.

WAR DIARY
or
INTELLIGENCE SUMMARY.
(Erase heading not required.)

Instructions regarding War Diaries and Intelligence Summaries are contained in F. S. Regs., Part II. and the Staff Manual respectively. Title pages will be prepared in manuscript.

Place	Date	Hour	Summary of Events and Information	Remarks and references to Appendices
MOYENVILLE	21 Jany		Company training. Weather fine.	J. Reid/H
"	22 Jany		Weather fine. 3" Div. G.S. 15/386 received. 3" Div. G/O. 212 Received reference move to HENIN. Reconnoitring positions to be taken over by Company.	J. Reid/H
"	23 Jany		Company training. Weather fine. Evacuations. 1.O.R. 1st C.C.S. 1 O.R. to Base. 1 O.R. to absence in U.K.	J. Reid/H
"	24 Jany		Company training. Coy D/O. No 21. reference move to HENIN.	J. Reid/H
HENIN	25 Jany		Moved camp to HENIN. Weather fine	J. Reid/H
"	26 Jany		Company employed on fatigues for Tunnellers 181st Tunnelling Coy. and constructing supplacements. Weather fine	J. Reid/H
"	27 Jany		Do. Do.	J. Reid/H

Army Form C. 2118.

WAR DIARY
or
INTELLIGENCE SUMMARY.
(Erase heading not required.)

Instructions regarding War Diaries and Intelligence Summaries are contained in F. S. Regs., Part II. and the Staff Manual respectively. Title pages will be prepared in manuscript.

Place	Date	Hour	Summary of Events and Information	Remarks and references to Appendices
HENIN	1918 28 Jany		Company employed on fatigues with 181 Tunnelling Coy and wiring party replacements.	L. Reid
"	29 Jany		No 2 Section moved to Defence line at HENINEL. No 4 Section moved to Defence line at CROISILLES. Situation Normal.	L. Reid
"	30 Jany		No 3 Section took up positions 2 guns at Post C.10 and 2 guns at post C.7 in Defence line.	L. Reid
"	31 Jany		Weather fine but cold. Situation quiet. Section Rain up at Boisleux Camp.	L. Reid

Confidential.

War Diary.

of

233rd Machine Gun Company.

From 1st February 1918.   To. 28th February 1918.

(Volume 4.)

Army Form C. 2118.

WAR DIARY
or
INTELLIGENCE SUMMARY.
(Erase heading not required.)

Instructions regarding War Diaries and Intelligence Summaries are contained in F. S. Regs., Part II. and the Staff Manual respectively. Title pages will be prepared in manuscript.

Place	Date	Hour	Summary of Events and Information	Remarks and references to Appendices
HENIN N32A33	1918 1st Feb.		Weather cold - misty. Section in Camp Training. Situation quiet.	Recces!
	2 Feb.		Weather fine. Section in Camp on fatigue. Situation in line quiet.	F. Rudolph
	3 Feb.		Weather fine. Section training at Details. Situation in line normal. Sec. Lt. W.L. SAMS returned from leave to U.K.	
	4 Feb.		Reinforcements 3 O.R. from Base. Weather fine. Section training at Details camp. Situation in line normal.	F. Rudolph
	5 Feb.		do do	F. Rudolph F. Rudolph
	6 Feb.		do do. Sec Lt. C.T. SMITH on leave to U.K. Evac: 1 O.R. to C.C.S.	F. Rudolph

Army Form C.2118.

WAR DIARY
or
INTELLIGENCE SUMMARY.
(Erase heading not required.)

Instructions regarding War Diaries and Intelligence Summaries are contained in F. S. Regs., Part II. and the Staff Manual respectively. Title pages will be prepared in manuscript.

Place	Date	Hour	Summary of Events and Information	Remarks and references to Appendices
HENIN	7Th.		Lectures training &c details	
			Situation normal	
			Evac. 1 OR. to C.C.S.	1. Field.
	8 Feb.		Weather Wet.	
			Situation normal	2. Field.
			Evac: 1 OR to BASE	
	9 Feb.		Weather fine	
			Situation normal	1. Field.
			Reinf! 1 OR (cook) from BASE	
	10 Feb.		Weather fine	
			Section training & details	1. Field.
			Situation normal	1. Field.
	11 Feb.		do do	
			Evac. 1 OR. to C.C.S	1. Field.
	12 Feb.		do do	
			Evac. 1 OR to C.C.S.	1. Field.
	13 Feb.		do do	
			Reinf! 3 OR from 12 OR. L.R. 1 OR. 15 7" K.S.L.I.	1. Field.
	14 Feb.		do do	
			Evac. 1 OR. to C.C.S. 1 to Z.A. over 7 days	1. Field.

WAR DIARY
or
INTELLIGENCE SUMMARY.

(Erase heading not required.)

Army Form C. 2118.

Place	Date	Hour	Summary of Events and Information	Remarks and references to Appendices
HENIN.	15th.		Weather fine. Situation in line normal. Section training at Aerails. Reinf: 5 O.R. from Base 2 Boredoulon Evac: 1 O.R. 15 C.C.S.	J. Reid Lt
	16. Feb.		do Reinf: 2 O.R. Htgtrs. Evac: 2 O.R. 15 C.C.S.	J. Reid Lt
	17th		do Reinf: 2 O.R. 13 R.L.R. 2 O.R. 15 T.N. 7s. 2 O.R. R.F. do	J. Reid Lt
	18th.		do	J. Reid Lt
	19th.		2nd Lt. A.R. WAUGH 15 T.U.R. leave. Evac: 1 O.R. m F.A. over 7 days Do Do No 1 Section to Dig Emplacements for Battery at 35 A.2.4. Training attached men at Aerails.	J. Reid Lt
	20 Feb.		Weather Wet. No 1 section digging Battery position. Training attached men. Reinf: 6 O.R. from K.S.L.I.	J. Reid Lt

Army Form C. 2118.

WAR DIARY
or
INTELLIGENCE SUMMARY.

(Erase heading not required.)

Instructions regarding War Diaries and Intelligence Summaries are contained in F.S. Regs., Part II. and the Staff Manual respectively. Title pages will be prepared in manuscript.

Place	Date	Hour	Summary of Events and Information	Remarks and references to Appendices
HENIN.	21 Feb.		Weather fine. No selective shelling. Rallying positions & dugouts a-taught. Training attached men. Situation quiet. Recpt. 11 O.R. from Base. Evac. 1 O.R. (15th Bordens) to C.C.S.	J. Riddell
	22 Feb.		do. Evac. 1 O.R. to C.C.S.	J. Riddell
	23 Feb.		do. Sec. Lt. C.T. SMITH M.C. returned from leave to U.K.	J. Riddell
	24 Feb.		Weather fine but colder. Formation of 3 M.G. Batt'n. Recpt. 1 O.R. from R.O.R.L.R. 1 O.R. from K.L.R. 1 O.R. rejoined from F.A. Evac. 1 O.R. to 18th R. O.R.L.R. Taken of strength (Nov.) the unproved Batt'n H.Q. Maj. MacKenzie & 2 O.R.	J. Riddell

Army Form C.2118.

WAR DIARY
or
INTELLIGENCE SUMMARY.
(Erase heading not required.)

Instructions regarding War Diaries and Intelligence Summaries are contained in F. S. Regs., Part II. and the Staff Manual respectively. Title pages will be prepared in manuscript.

Place	Date	Hour	Summary of Events and Information	Remarks and references to Appendices
HENIN	25th Feb		Weather fine. Section attached new heavy arterials. Situation normal.	J. Tulloch
	26th Feb		Weather variable. Section attached new heavy arterials. Situation normal.	J. Tulloch
	27th Feb		do. do.	J. Tulloch
	28th Feb		Weather cold. Section attached new tramway arterials. Situation normal.	J. Tulloch